Time at the Lake
A Minnesota Album

by
William Albert Allard

Pfeifer-Hamilton Publishers
Duluth, Minnesota

Pfeifer-Hamilton Publishers
210 West Michigan
Duluth MN 55802-1908
218-727-0500

Time at the Lake: A Minnesota Album

Printed by Doosan Dong-A Co., Ltd.
10 9 8 7 6 5 4 3 2 1

Editorial Director: Donald A. Tubesing
Art Director: Joy Morgan Dey

Library of Congress Cataloging in Publication Data
Allard, William Albert.
    Time at the lake : a Minnesota album / by William Albert Allard.
    128 p. 23 cm.
    ISBN 1-57025-133-9
    1. Lakes—Minnesota. 2. Minnesota—Description and travel.
  3. Minnesota—Pictorial works. 4. Minnesota—Social life and customs.
  5. Allard, William Albert—Childhood and youth.
  I. Title.
  F612.A18A45 1997
  977.6—dc21   97-21099
                            12-26-97   CIP

Printed in Republic of Korea

Alluring Pines Resort, Lake Hubert

Acknowledgments

My thanks first of all to all who appear in the photographs, whether by request or by chance. Very often the best pictures are not taken, but given. Thanks also to the following people and organizations, who are in one way or another a part of this book:

To everyone at Pfeifer-Hamilton Publishers. To Marianne Samenko of Eastman Kodak Company and to Peter Fitzgerald of Qualex Incorporated for their support with film and processing. To the National Geographic Society for accepting my proposal six years ago to produce an article about the Minnesota lake country, an idea I had harbored in my mind for years but had never proposed for fear of being suspected by my friends of simply wanting to go fishing. In truth, my fishing abilities have never been very good, certainly not worthy of a book. But then, this book isn't really about fishing.

To R. Smith "Smitty" Schuneman for his unfailing guidance, advice, and affection for over half my life and his.

To all those who probably should be in this book but for some reason are not. To Larren Wood, owner of Fremont's Point Resort on Mantrap Lake, for her encouragement to do this book. To Jim Wentworth of Fish Lectronics in Nisswa, a guy from Iowa who's so nice you'd think he'd been born in Minnesota. To Willis and Martha Unke, to Weezie and Janene, and all the family members who own Kee-Nee-Moo-Sha Resort on Woman Lake, where I spent much time. To Jack and Beulah Szabo, the former owners of Oak Grove, the last resort on Gladstone Lake. The weather was bad the day I interviewed them, and I didn't photograph them, thinking there would be another opportunity. When I looked for them four years later I found they'd moved somewhere out of the state to be closer to their kids.

To my wife, Ani, who loves to fish and regularly does so better than I, for her love and loyalty. And a special thanks to my youngest son, Anthony, now nine. In one of our frequent long-distance telephone conversations I told him of some event I was going to see and photograph in the country in which I was working at the time. "Oh, Papi," he said, "You're lucky every day." Thank you, Anthony, for reminding me of that.

Driftwood Resort, Upper Whitefish Lake

George Allard, Gladstone Lake, 1928

*This book is dedicated
to the memory of my father and mother,
George and Willie Allard, who started our
family's lake tradition so very many years ago.*

*For my sister, Ann DeGray,
my brother, Bruce, and my late brother, Bob.*

*And for my children, Scott, Chris,
Terri, David, and Anthony.*

*May all future generations of our family
be blessed with memories of Minnesota waters.*

North of the stress zone

There are those who say they go to the Minnesota lake country to fish and relax. I think that's redundant. A lot of people do go there to fish, of course. But perhaps more than anything else, people go to the lake country to relax, whether by fishing, water-skiing, hauling each other around on inflatable tubes behind fast-moving boats, dreaming away afternoons on a plastic mattress in a couple of feet of water, or getting buried in a book after dark on a cabin porch screened off from mosquitoes but not the outdoors and the sounds of loons and of water lapping at a lake's edge. Whatever the choice, the goal is to be, as a sign at the entrance to a Deer River resort proclaims, "north of the stress zone."

I have an old and battered photograph album with snapshots of my parents, made when they were first married. There are pictures of them taken on trips from the city to Brainerd. There is a picture of a Model T with small American flags mounted on the headlamps. The car is what I think they called a "touring" model, with open sides and a retractable canvas top. One photograph shows my father on a dock with a five- or six-pound northern on a stringer. My father wears knee-high lace-up leather boots. He is handsome and young. In another picture my father stands with a friend on the shore of a lake, a narrow-beamed rowboat behind them. Between them they hold a stringer with about twenty fish. Walleyes and northerns. In pencil, along the edges of the photograph, my mother wrote: "Our last day at Gladstone. Enough for breakfast."

My family spent parts of sixty summers going to the same small lake in the Brainerd area—in what could be called the heart of the state's north-central lake area. We stayed at a variety of mom-and-pop owned resorts over the years, the last one a cluster of rustic cabins nestled in a grove of middle-aged oaks.

I was twenty-six when I moved out east thirty-two years ago following graduation from

My family spent parts of sixty summers going to the same small lake in the Brainerd area—in what could be called the heart of the state's north-central lake area.

the University of Minnesota. My work as a freelance photographer and writer kept me drifting around the world, but still touching base in Minneapolis whenever possible, sometimes managing to get up north with my young family, my siblings, and our parents, although those times became less frequent as we all grew older and our lives slid off in different directions. The lives of my parents seemed anchored in a regularity and permanence that I wanted to avoid in my own. I had become a traveler. I had a permanent address but I wasn't there about half of each year. Love for travel, the unfamiliar, and my work was in constant conflict with love for family and home, for the familiar and traditional. That conflict still exists. Besides love for people to whom you are closest, there can exist an equally strong love for a place, a house, a city, or a piece of country; and when you have to be away from both or all, it's not easy, no matter how deep your passion for other matters such as work, no matter how great your dedication to that work.

Although seemingly more heavily used each year, the heart of the Minnesota lake country—the easily accessible region within three to five hours of the Twin Cities—is still what it's always been in one way or another to so many people: something for the heart and mind that goes beyond explanation. You can go away and for years not see those woods, or feel the winds blowing off those lakes, or put a toe into their waters, and yet still carry them with you. If you knew those things at their best and yours, as a child, that kind of country becomes a part of you always.

For a few years as a kid I had a chance for more lake time than usual because I had an aunt and uncle with a lake home in Wisconsin. When I was eleven and twelve I lived there for a few weeks each summer. They had some chickens,

Years later I learned how to filet those Y bones away, leaving as fine a tasting piece of fresh water fish as anything that swims, short, perhaps, of a plateful of butter-fried bluegills.

ducks, a few sheep, and a record collection that included Gershwin's "Rhapsody in Blue," a different kind of music from what I was accustomed to at home. Their lake was full of juvenile northern pike—"hammer handles," as my short, cigar-smoking Uncle Ted called them—ferocious freshwater thugs that weren't difficult to catch, even for an eleven-year-old. I'd get them on a red and white spoon, one of only a handful of lures I possessed at that stage of my life. The energy of the strikes and the struggles of those one-pound terrorists were what made fishing exciting to me. Most people, of course, looked down on them: too many bones. Years later I learned how to filet those Y bones away, leaving as fine a tasting piece of freshwater fish as anything that swims, short, perhaps, of a plateful of butter-fried bluegills.

My big bosomy Aunt Lydia was into seances and cleaning the house while talking to people who weren't there. When I wasn't doing chores for Aunt Lydia—she didn't trust me much with weeding around the house because I'd take too heavy a toll on her flower beds—I was fishing from the rowboat or down around the dock. I spent a lot of time on that dock, sometimes indulging in those curious cruelties of which kids are capable, dissecting hostage frogs with a pocketknife, leaving their carcasses floating, white bellies up, in the water.

I can remember the smell of my uncle's cigar that was always jammed into his mouth or gripped between his fingers, and how cigar ash speckled the front of the white undershirt he wore on hot summer nights out on the screened porch, playing cards with adult friends, a fog of pungent smoke hanging yellow-gray beneath the porch light, a bottle of some kind of Wisconsin beer standing sentry on the floor by the legs of his folding chair. I remember the times he'd stop the car on a quiet country road going home from town and walk into some farmer's field like those ball players in the movie *Field of Dreams*. After a few minutes he'd come back out, a short man made seemingly shorter by the awkward armload of sweet corn that made him hunch over as he scurried quickly to the car to dump the loot on the backseat next to me. I remember how the yellow-tassled ears smelled like summer.

It's funny, if in retrospect totally understandable, how we can remember smells of childhood, when the olfactory senses were birth-given sharp, before adult vices dulled them. The smells can be so specific and become so imbedded in our memories, recalling places and periods in our young lives. Like how the skunky-smelling iron-laced water from the faucet above the resort cabin sink, with its reddish brown stains ringing the porcelain edge of the drain, assaulted the nose each time I raised a glass to drink or smothered my face with a washrag. And the essence of decay that came with hauling up an anchor entangled with cabbage weeds and heavy with clumps of mud and muck from the lake's bottom. Long after the last marshmallow had been roasted, the night's breeze brought the acrid edge of the dying bonfire in through the screen window of the cabin.

And of course there were the smells of the city and home. The sweet oily asphalt fragrance that clung to our shoes and bicycle tires after a hot summer afternoon of hanging around the blacktopping crew working our street in north Minneapolis, where I grew up in a house on the edge of Camden, when Camden was on the far north edge of the city. Like most family homes that have been lived in for very long, ours had a variety of smells. There was the smell, a bit musty, of the pages of the old illustrated world history books I'd pull from our few bookshelves, and the smell of the living room carpet I sprawled on to look at the pictures. And the smell of linseed oil in the back entryway where my father hung his jacket. If you came in at night, through the back door, into the kitchen, that area had its own smell, for some reason more distinct at night. Our unfinished basement had a damp and musty smell, with accents of wood shavings and paint or stain. And laundry. Other parts had their own smells.

Places that are truly lived in are like that. Like the homes of old women who live alone. As a boy I cut the grass and did small chores for an elderly woman who lived across the alley from us. Mrs. Costello was a kind old widow, bent, gray-haired, and frail, and sometimes her house smelled of cookies; but more often her house had a smell that always kept me from feeling comfortable and made me want to get outside. It smelled of age, I guess, an oldness that was more than musty.

Garages have their own identities too, especially older ones—automotive smells from the gasoline and oil that stains the concrete apron; the aroma of unfinished pine boards and two by fours, lumber from the thirties and forties when a two by four was truly that. In our neighborhood the garages were all unattached, small square structures connected to the houses by a narrow strip of sidewalk woven through modest backyards and gardens.

Fifteen years ago my older brother, Bob, took his own life in my parents' garage, the same garage where over the years my father had racked upon the rafters the fishing poles of summer. My mother found him there in his car, key in the ignition, on a Memorial Day afternoon, traditionally the start of the summer season. It wasn't gruesome, she told me later; he could have been sleeping. Why my brother chose to do what he did, when and where he did it, I really don't know. He was in his mid-fifties when he died, and maybe life had taken on a smell of oldness that made him want to get outside of it. I can sometimes understand that.

I guess I can also understand why my father settled for pan fishing at an early age. Easy fish to catch, they didn't really present a challenge, and they were sweet eating, if indeed bony. The pictures I have of him with a nice northern and a fine string of walleyes were made in the 1920s when he was in his twenties. I was born in 1937, when he was thirty-eight. Maybe it had something to do with going through the Depression years; maybe that took away his sense of adventure as it did to so many, although my father was never out of work, which was then as a baker of Swedish flatbread. (He later took a job in a linseed mill for harder but better-paying work.) But for as long as I knew him, or at least can recollect positively, my father fished only for sunnies and crappies. Never northerns, never bass, and, almost heretical to admit, as a Minnesotan—never walleyes. Sunnies and crappies. Still fishing.

My thoughts, as a boy, however, were of bass smashing up through lily pads, exploding out of the water in a way to make your heart skip, a brightly colored plug dangling precariously from the gaping mouth by the single barb of a glistening treble hook. I had visions, timeless as dreams, of strong northern pike— "northerns"—the perfect name for Minnesota's lethally beautiful fish, a kind of light-heavyweight champion of the lakes, slightly in the shadow of the muskie. I wanted to catch the fish that I saw on the covers of the hunting and fishing magazines that lay on the floor by the side of my father's chair in the living room of that house in Camden. He, for some reason, didn't, but I did. I realized years later that it wasn't important what he fished for; what was most important is that he took us to the lake. And that is what this book is about. Going to the lake. It's about the smells and the sounds. And some of the people who live there.

In 1991, after years away from northern Minnesota, I returned to write and photograph an article on the north-central lake country for *National Geographic*. I returned again, for myself (although the time spent there for the magazine was really for me too) with my family for parts of the last few summers. The pictures and the words in this book are drawn from those days when I went looking for pieces of my past. I found some, but I'm still looking, and for as long as I can, I intend to keep going back to look for more.

Kee-Nee-Moo-Sha Resort, Woman Lake
Longville, Minnesota
August 1996

I realized years later that it wasn't important what he fished for; what was most important is that he took us to the lake.

Birch Villa Resort, Cass Lake

Birch Villa Resort, Cass Lake

A special world

I grew up surrounded by water, or so it seemed. Although none of it was usually in immediate view, I always knew it was there just by looking at the license plate on my father's car. Sometimes on Sundays we'd drive up to visit my Uncle Hank, who farmed a quarter-section of sandy soil near Isanti, north of Minneapolis. After a big, country-style dinner of fried chicken, ham, and maybe some Swedish sausage, cooked on a woodstove that scented the old farm house with aromas of food and fire, my mother and my Aunt Margaret would wash the dishes and tend to the kitchen, while my father and his brother stood outside the house by their cars, talking about crops and my father's work at the linseed mill in the city. In tieless white shirts with sleeves rolled up to their elbows, they drank beer from amber-colored long-necked bottles. They'd stand with one foot resting on a car bumper and there,

Nothing seemed difficult, and there was always a second chance.

framed by the toes of their Sunday shoes, was the description of the place we lived:

> **Minnesota**
> Land of 10,000 Lakes

When we returned home in the evenings, that tin license plate was the last thing I would see when my father shut the garage door. A land of ten thousand lakes. It was hard to imagine. It still is.

Today, more than four decades later, Minnesota license plates still carry that description, although it is no more accurate now then it was when the state first adopted the slogan in 1950. I discovered relatively late in life that Minnesota actually has more than 15,000 lakes, varying in size from ten acres to those best described in terms of miles across. Minnesota has more shoreline than

California, Florida, and Hawaii combined. Although they're scattered throughout the state, the greatest concentration of these lakes—most of them formed by the departure of the glacier age—are found a few hours' drive north of the Twin Cities. There, in north-central Minnesota, lies the heart of the lake country.

It was there that my family rented a lake cabin for one week each summer. We didn't go to just any lake, of course, but, as so many Minnesotans have done all their lives, we went to *the* lake, in our case, Gladstone, a quiet 400-acre lake in Nisswa, near Brainerd. My parents first went there in the 1920s, when they were young and just married. Their car was a Model T Ford and the roads were not much more than graveled cow paths. For sixty summers our family would return to Gladstone, staying at a number of different mom-and-pop resorts over the decades. It was there, swimming and fishing, exploring the shoreline and enduring the mosqui-

toes one could never truly escape, that I came to love the lake country in that special way one loves as a child.

The lake was my own special world for one week each year of my boyhood. Not nearly so far away from my home in Minneapolis as I envisioned it to be, it was far enough from the confines of the city to make me crave to be there, where the pines were towering and the forest deep. I wanted to run to the dock in early morning, when sunlight glistened off the dew-covered boards as if they were inlaid with diamonds. I wanted to see what creatures had passed along the water's edge while I had slept, leaving their footprints as calling cards for my imagination. That week that promised to last forever brought laughter and stories to tell when it was over, which was always too soon. As a friend of mine put it, nothing seemed difficult, and there was always a second chance.

Gull Lake

18

TIME AT THE LAKE

Opening day, Judd's Resort, Lake Winnibigoshish

Opening day: in pursuit of fish

If it's possible for the population of a state to have a love affair with a fish, Minnesota has had a torrid and long-lasting one with the walleye. Minnesota has more walleyes and more walleye lakes than any other state. Each spring on a Saturday around the middle of May a million anglers go out in pursuit of this fish.

They come from all over the state and beyond; they come from Iowa, Kansas, Illinois, Nebraska, and the Dakotas, clogging the two-lane highways with caravans of boat-laden trailers, lots of them heading for the big walleye lakes—Leech, Winnibigoshish, and the "factory"—Mille Lacs Lake. Bait shops stay open around the clock; all the resorts are full, and there are no motel rooms to be found. It's opening day.

Almost half of Minnesota's lakes are considered fishable, and more than a million and a half fishing licenses are sold annually. That in-cludes about four hundred thousand nonresidents, but it does not include kids under sixteen, who aren't required to buy a license. A northern Minnesota newspaper reported that a recent study indicated 97 percent of all kids in Minnesota go fishing. "That's deplorable," said the newspaper. "What on earth went wrong with that other 3 percent."

At Swanson's in Hackensack, LeRoy's up in Cass Lake, Reed's in Walker, the famous Marv Koeps's down in Nisswa, and countless other bait shops, opening-day fishermen crowd around, digging through the bins, feeling the weight of lead-head jigs in the palm of the hand, and the prick of treble hooks on colorful lures that hang from racks like Christmas tree ornaments. Night crawlers and leeches in round white containers stand stacked in coolers like towers of yogurt or cottage cheese. Thousands of minnows, from tiny ones to some that look big enough to make a meal, are scooped by the flip-flopping silvered dozens from water tanks gurgling with aerators and emptied into plastic bags injected with blasts of oxygen to get them from the bait shop to the minnow bucket in the boat. And everywhere around are the fish-tempters, offered in fluorescent colors and odd shapes that don't always seem to look like something a fish might want to eat, but that the manufacturers claim are irresistible. Better buy a couple of these, you think, and often do.

In the silver-blue light of dawn of opening day, I walked down to the harbor from my Judd's Resort cabin on Lake Winnibigoshish, the shallow, 69,000-acre bowl of water known as "Big Winnie." There were already a few empty slips, left vacant by fishermen who had headed out in the darkness of night. The other boats, several dozen or so, rested quietly, sheltered by a breakwater of earth and rocks that embraced the harbor in the crook of its arm.

In groups of two or three, fishermen came down to the docks, carrying yellow minnow buckets and coffee thermoses, fishing rods and tackle boxes. Nobody talked much. It was early. One at a time the boats left the harbor, moving slowly out through the shallow channel, trailing no wake until they reached deeper water. There they opened their throttles; some turned off to the north and some ran straight toward where the sun would rise. Within minutes their shapes and sounds were engulfed and silenced by water and space.

One evening during opening day weekend at Judd's, I shared in a fish dinner cooked by outdoor writer Ron Schara. Schara and a collection of his brothers and uncles gather at a different

It was early.
One at a time the boats left the harbor, moving slowly out through the shallow channel, trailing no wake until they reached deeper water.

lake each year to celebrate opening day together. A lot of kidding flew back and forth among the all-male clan; and because some of them had originally lived in Iowa, and others still did, they brought out the usual timeworn Iowa jokes common in northern Minnesota.

"Yeah, old Uncle Charlie came to Minnesota from Iowa," said Schara, with a grin. "You know, he came here with one extra pair of underwear and a two dollar bill, and he hasn't changed either one since."

Schara talked about how important the opening day of fishing season is to the people of Minnesota. "I don't think any other state has the same kind of enthusiasm for opening day," he said. "The entire state gets up for it. People who *never* fish come out on opening day. Of course, it's easier to get up north today than it used to be. Used to be all gravel roads, and it

was a commitment to come up this far north, beyond Brainerd. That's just an hour or so closer to the city, but when the roads were bad that was enough to make this country seem a bit too far. It's not too far anymore."

In the fish house at Judd's I asked a man who was cleaning fish with his son if he thought the fishing has changed over the years. They live farther south, near the cities.

"Oh, yeah," he said. "We've been coming up here for twenty years and we've been on Big Winnie when it was crazy. You couldn't keep 'em off the hook. It's not like it used to be. But, you know, down where we live you can't hardly get on a lake this time of year. Hell, they sank a boat down there a couple of years ago. They were running into each other."

Driving around after dark, I stopped at a cafe in a tiny community on the south edge of

Big Winnie. It was the kind of place where meals come with big scoops of real butter and a dessert, whether you want it or not. The waitress was chatting with four men drinking beer and looking at their menus. She was telling them about a difficult woman customer who'd been in earlier.

"So, I said to her, 'What's your problem, lady?' And she says to me, 'Three kids and a husband.' " The waitress looked at the men and rolled her eyes in mock disgust.

"Now, are you guys gonna order so I can get outta here?"

A small boy came in to the cafe and was complaining about the slowness of summer arriving. "I can't wait til I get out of school," he said. "Why?" asked the waitress. "What are you gonna do?"

"Go fishin'," he replied. "Go fishin'."

In the cabins back at Judd's men were sitting around tables, and on the edges of their beds, talking. "Some of us have been fishing partners for years," one of them told me. "This is a place we can go to get away from the things that might be bothering us. This is a time when we can talk about problems in our work and in our marriages. For some of us it's the only time and place we do that."

In the morning they will go out again to fish. And to talk.

Opening day, Judd's Resort, Lake Winnibigoshish

Opening day, Lake Winnibigoshish

Dick Grzywinski
fishing guide

Anthony's first northern, Kee-Nee-Moo-Sha Resort, Woman Lake

Resort owners, Ann and Ed Davis

Ann and Ed Davis, both in their sixties, run Boberg's Cottages and Motel, a Gull Lake resort Ann's father started in 1924. Their cabins are modest and probably haven't changed much over the years. I felt very much at home in mine. I grew fond of watching Ann sprightly walking the grounds, checking out the kids, and Ed riding his old balloon-tired bicycle or driving his '68 blunt-nosed Dodge truck.

In the summer of 1991, while staying at Boberg's, I talked with Ann and Ed and Ann's sixty-one-year-old brother, Carl, in the Davises' living room, dominated by a Swedish grandfather's clock and other odds and ends that reflected the old country. Ann brought out ice cream, delicious chocolate cake, and coffee. In Swedish cups, of course. "Swedes can never serve just coffee," she said, laughing.

"The four original resorts of Gull Lake were run by Swedes," Ann told me. "Some of the first were just tents on wood platforms."

Raised on the resort, Ann and Carl remember how hard their parents had to work to support the business. "When we were growing up we spent most of our time running from Mom and Dad," said Carl. "They drove us so hard because there was so much work to do around the resort. We didn't have lawn mowers. We cut the grass with scythes. We finally got a lawn mower after World War Two. With a motor. I couldn't believe it."

"We still do all the work ourselves," said Ann. "You can't afford to hire help."

The Davises have seen their clientele's interest change over the years. "In the 1930s we'd get a big bunch of people from Kansas City, the Chevy motor gang, and a judge from Oklahoma . . . very serious fishermen," said Ann. "And in those days you could just walk across the fish. But it's always hard to deal with people who are fishermen if for some reason they aren't catching fish. It's terribly hard. They just hammer on you."

"We don't get as many fishermen now. We're getting more families, the children and grandchildren of people who first came here years ago. And, of course, now we're getting single-parent families."

The Davises and Carl Boberg have watched the number of resorts on Gull Lake decline over the years.

"I could take you around Gull and show you," said Carl. "There was so and so, there was so and so, just one after another resort on this lake that isn't there anymore."

"We'd wonder every year, how many went out this year?" I mention a man I'd met who had said he wanted to retire early and run a resort in northern Minnesota.

"We've seen that dream shattered many times," said Carl.

"They only stay two or three years and then the taxes get them," said Ann.

"Our dad used to say, 'A resort isn't a business, it's a way of life,' " said Carl.

"And that's what it is. It's a family way of life, and you just stick around and kind of like it. But financially it's a disaster. Compared to what the real estate is worth today."

It's been estimated that 60 percent of Minnesota's resort business is in the Brainerd area. "That ribbon of highway out there," said Carl, nodding toward the front of the house that sits hard on the edge of Highway 371, "we think of it as the gold coast."

"That's where all the money comes up.

Our dad used to say, 'A resort isn't a business, it's a way of life.'

Tourists. Our dad used to call them 'foreign aid.' "

I stopped at Boberg's one August morning fours years later to make a portrait of Ann and Ed. She was as perky as ever, Ed was his mop-haired, dry-witted self. Before we went outside to find a place to make the pictures we had coffee, of course, with some homemade sweet rolls. Outside, in the crisp early morning light, I photographed them standing in the grass beneath the trees and also on the dock. The resort was quiet, no one else was up yet, at least not outside, and yesterdays's toys, inflated tubes and water skis, lay abandoned in front of the cabins.

"How about something warm and intimate," I said, kidding them. They each put an arm around each other and grinned. "You know what a Swedish kiss is, don't you?" asked Ann. "A handshake." Then I reminded her about the Swede who loved his wife so much he almost told her. Having grown up with a Swedish father, I knew what I was talking about.

Ann and Ed Davis, owners, Boberg's Cottages and Motel, Gull Lake

Boberg's Cottages and Motel, Gull Lake

Madsen Grove Resort, Little Floyd Lake

Bambi Resort, Lake Hubert

Kee-Nee-Moo-Sha Resort, Woman Lake

Resort owner, Vera Kinder

Vera Kinder is seventy-seven and has run Forest View Resort on Leech Lake for forty-six years, forty of them with her husband, Orville. They came to Minnesota from Kansas in the early 1950s and fell in love with the north country. Like all long-term resort owners, Vera's seen the business change over the years. Not exactly a mom-and-pop operation, Forest View has seventeen cabins and a lodge with a bar and restaurant.

"It used to be just fish 'em, feed 'em, and sleep 'em. We never had too many kids, and now we have sixty a week. Used to be guests would use fishing guides. The guides would sit down on the dock, just waiting for clients to take out. Now everybody's got their own boat. And now there's golf and horseback riding for those who might not want to fish."

After all the years she's been running the resort, Vera's love for the place and the lake remains. "Every time Orville and I took a trip—when we came back, we'd stand in the yard and think, 'My God, how beautiful this is.'"

Vera Kinder, owner, Forest View Resort, Leech Lake

Gull Lake

Lake Wasson

Leech Lake

Big Rock Resort, Leech Lake

A bunch of old boys, Nisswa Cafe

If you hang around lake country coffee shops and restaurants on early mornings you hear some funny stuff. It's the kind of humor that comes when neighbors are friends and see each other nearly every day through good times and bad. The talk is dry and sharp, honed by living where the climate, at least in winter, requires a good sense of humor.

A bunch of older men, five of them, are sitting at their regular table near the cash register in the Country Cookin' Cafe in Nisswa. A well-tanned man sits down near them on a stool at the end of the counter. "Hi, Al," greets one of the guys at the table. "What's happening?"

"There's a lot happening," replies Al, "I just haven't figured out what it is yet."

"Oh, yeah?"

"Yeah," says Al. "Sometimes it takes me until noon."

A sixth man joins the group at the table. He's tall, fair-skinned, and appears to be in his late sixties or early seventies. From his jacket pocket he takes a partly used jar of strawberry jelly and places it on the table. "Jeez," says one of the guys, "why don't you bring your own toast, too?"

"Why don't you go back to Iowa?" replies the man with the jelly. "Don't they have any eggs in Iowa?"

"That's probably where they all come from," says another.

"How many people bring their own jelly?" asks the guy who brought up the subject.

"Never mind, we're not talking to you."

"God, this is a good group," says one of them to the waitress who's come over with coffee. "We just love each other."

I ask the waitress about the guy bringing

his own jelly and she tells me he has a choles-
terol problem. "We tell him if he doesn't like ours,
to bring his own."

Wherever you find these bunches of old
buddies gathered together, it's like coming upon
the Seven Dwarfs on coffee break. There always
seems to be a Happy, a Dopey, and you can rest
assured, there will be a Grumpy, too.

Two women in bar in Floodwood

At a bar and restaurant in Floodwood, in the north woods between Duluth and Grand Rapids, bear, wolf, and coyote pelts drape the log walls behind the elderly woman selling pulltabs—at half a buck or a dollar a crack, the multicolored paper debris that litters bar tops and floors of places throughout Minnesota.

The rest of the walls are covered with trophy heads of deer, elk, and moose, and rows of antlers mounted on wood with small brass plaques that say who shot what and when. One corner of the rectangular bar is lined with working men in working mens' dirty T-shirts and scuffed and sweat-marked baseball caps. A huge construction worker in a sleeveless T-shirt that says simply "DESTROYERS" stands literally belly up to the bar. His arms, which are very large, are covered with tattoos that are just as large.

I am trying to read Rick Bass's book *Winter* and also eavesdrop, as best I can, on the conversation moving along the bar like waves. It is early evening, around the end of Happy Hour. Two women next to me at the bar busy themselves opening pulltabs, lining them up in front of them next to their drinks and cigarette packs. The women, the older appearing to be in her early forties and the other somewhere in her thirties, are dressed in Easter-egg colors. The older one wears a bright green skirt and jacket. The younger woman has on an equally bright pink jacket, unbuttoned over a black jersey. She is what one might call full-breasted.

At the other end of the bar are several blondes, real and otherwise. One of them has a lovely child-woman face and wears her sunglasses hanging from the neck of her T-shirt, tugging down the neckline. Her hair is an impossible white blonde, not quite platinum. She is maybe twenty. A few feet away the big construction worker stands at the edge of light angling down from a spot above the bar. The light falls on his heavily tattooed upper arm. These are not timid tattoos but broad, large-lettered announcements: U.S. ARMY is perfectly visible to me sitting twenty feet away.

The bartender picks up handfuls of discarded pulltabs, and I ask the woman in Easter-egg green if maybe it's possible to become addicted to these small ventures of chance. "Yeah, it's addictive," she says grinning, "just like any gambling." A pack of Marlboro Lights rests on the bar next to her drink. She holds a single pulltab between her slender fingers. "This is my last one," she says. "Where did they all go?"

"Five hundred!" she screams. "Five hundred!" With her last pulltab, Easter-egg green has won five hundred dollars. She and Easter-egg pink embrace excitely. "Oh, God," says the winner, "I said I was gonna hit it and I said I was gonna choke on my own saliva when I did. Oh, God! Anybody here know CPR?"

"No," says a man in his sixties, sitting one stool over. "But for you I'll give it a try."

"You want anything to drink?" the woman in green asks her girlfriend.

"God! No!" says the woman in pink. "We should buy a round, though, I suppose."

Turns out they are friends from Duluth and share a love for pulltabs and always divide their winnings. And tomorrow is the birthday of the younger woman. "She's thirty-six tomorrow," says her friend. "It's her golden birthday 'cause her bust and her age are gonna be the same."

They do buy a round, and an old fella in a yellow shirt and brown suspenders thanks them profusely. A few minutes later the winner saunters over to the pulltabs with a ten-dollar bill in her hand. "Talk to me baby," she says, kissing the ten-spot.

"Come to Mama." Her swaying hips seem to approach the pulltab counter just a bit before the rest of her.

Annie's Cafe, Longville

46

Longville waitress

It is a cold, rainy morning in Longville. The rain comes down hard, slanted by the wind. In the window of Annie's Cafe the neon OPEN sign glows orange. Late August, the last couple of days of the last week of summer, but the harsh weather makes it seem like late September. The waitress wears a black knit sweater, and on her chest the perky face of Betty Boop surrounded by an array of small red hearts. She brings me coffee.

"How are ya doin'?" I ask.

"I'm doin' great," she says. "How about you?"

"Not so great. The weather could be better."

"You're not pregnant, are you?" she asks.

"No," I reply. "Are you?"

"No," she says, "so we're both doin' great."

I raise my camera to take a picture of her Betty Boop sweater and she protests.

"Trust me," I say.

"I don't trust anybody," she says. "especially if they've got one of those." But she lets me take the picture and I tell her that I'm working on a book about the area. This is what photographers sometimes do on rainy days, I think to myself, after she goes off with her coffee to tend other tables. We sit around drinking coffee, waiting for a picture to come by. Not that much different from fishing, I suppose.

Annie's Cafe, Longville

Polka Tavern, Cross Lake

Brainerd Jaycees Ice-Fishing Extravaganza, Gull Lake

50

Ice-fishing

When I was a boy, fishing was a summertime thing, at least in my family. We never went ice-fishing, and to this day I still haven't. We had a neighbor who sometimes went ice-fishing and when he came back he'd have buckets of frozen crappies sitting inside his garage—with the door open, of course, so the neighbors could witness his success. Some of us kids would stand in the alley, straddling the icy ruts of tire tracks, watching him count his fish, our woolen mittens, hand-knitted by our mothers, frozen solid at their tips from countless wipes of runny noses and slushball fights. When we got bored looking at frozen crappies, we'd go to a vacant lot at the end of the alley, where we'd play tackle football, our falls cushioned by snow that sometimes reached our hips.

Just about every lake in and around the city used to have a few ice-fishing houses sitting out there like lonely Arctic outposts. Now that people can reach the lakes whenever they feel like going, a lake as big as 132,000-acre Mille Lacs sprouts more than four thousand ice-fishing houses grouped in small villages across the snow-swept surface.

I once flew in a helicopter above Gull Lake on the January afternoon of the Brainerd Jaycees annual $100,000 Ice-Fishing Extravaganza. Below me more than five thousand hopeful fishermen and women darkened the snow in an area about one-third by one-half mile, where nine thousand holes had been drilled in the lake for the three-hour contest. Prizes included pickup trucks and a trip for two to Hawaii. From the air the assembled anglers looked like a page from one of those *Where's Waldo?* books for kids. I can only imagine what it must have looked like to a fish.

Each February the town of Walker hosts an eelpout festival on Leech Lake, as crazy an outdoor event as you might find anywhere. Some ten thousand people show up for the weekend, although it's pretty clear that many of them have no intention of putting a line in the water.

At dawn on the first day of the festival I watched four young men from the mainly Finnish town of Menahga trying to fire up a wood-burning stove to heat the water for their hot tub set up just outside their fish house, which was a beat-up mobile home with a bucket full of empty beer cans by the door. The men had arrived the night before, and all appeared in need of sleep.

Not satisfied with the stove's output, one of the young anglers decided to prime it a little by pouring some charcoal-starter fluid down the stovepipe. He got what a thinking person might expect—a small explosion out the end of the pipe and a hand that was considerably warmer than it had been. He jumped back, shaking his hand in great surprise. "Well, jeez," one of his buddies observed, "you spent a month down in Minneapolis. You'd think you'd know better."

Two of the other men were struggling to erect a banner identifying their spot as The Oasis, but just couldn't get it to hang straight and finally gave up. "That's close enough for the girls we go out with," one of them said.

Later that day I stopped again to see the hot tub bunch. They were all submerged in the water, drinking schnapps and beer while a few snowmobilers bundled up in their suits and helmets stood watching them like a crew of ice-stranded astronauts. Country music spilled out from the fish house. Merle Haggard on ice. One of the men in the tub made an effort at social grace by introducing his companions.

"I'll give you a little history of our group," he said, pointing out each man with a stick of firewood. "This is my brother-in-law, this is my brother-in-law, and this is my brother-in-law's brother-in-law." Having established the family tree, he lowered himself back into the steaming water, a shot glass dangling from his neck by a string.

The eelpout is not a pretty fish. Some fish are downright attractive, such as trout, walleye, and sunfish, especially the brilliantly colored pumpkinseed. Even muskies and northerns have a kind of lethal beauty. But not an eelpout. A member of the freshwater cod family, and the only fish to spawn in winter, the eelpout is flatheaded and potbellied, and seems to drip with slime. When held up for examination, it has a rather unnerving tendency to wrap its slimy tail around your forearm. While Minnesotans worship the walleye to a point just short of having a "blessing of the walleye," as folks do with fox-hounds in the South, most of them don't want an eelpout in their house, let alone their religion. But the "pout" does have admirers among those who truly like the taste of fish. The strip of meat along the back is considered, by those who know, to be delicious. I suppose it's a bit akin to kissing an ugly person in bright light: the effect may be just wonderful, but getting to it can be a trip.

At the festival weigh-in station people were looking at hundreds of frozen eelpout hanging from racks, their tails curled, as if in motion. "Oh, gross!" said a pretty girl who didn't look like the type to bait her own hook.

"God," uttered a woman, holding her hand up to her mouth in repulsion. "It's hard to be-lieve they came out of that beautiful lake."

"I actually went out there and caught one of those things last night," said a man wearing a hat made from a skunk and carrying a bottle of something wrapped in a brown paper bag. "Felt my IQ drop about thirty points."

Eelpout Festival, Leech Lake, Walker

Eelpout Festival, Leech Lake, Walker

Powwow

As a kid I always had a canoe around the house, a miniature one, about the length of a cigar and made from birchbark, something we bought at a roadside stand on the drive up to the lake one summer. At those souvenir places you could buy lots of simple crafts that reflected the region, such as birchbark canoes, little birchbark drums, and slices of pine with the bark still dark and flaky around the edges and, painted on the face of the wood under a honeyed glaze of varnish, some homily about nature or fishing or perhaps the name of a lake country town and a fact about it like "Little Falls, Minnesota, Home of Charles Lindberg." It might have a thermometer attached and advertise a resort. Or maybe it would show the face of an Indian.

I don't remember seeing any Indians when I was a child, but, of course, they were there. The Ojibwa were present when the first white explorers appeared in the 1600s. Some of the lakes and towns in this region, such as Bemidji, take their names from the Ojibwa. And the last armed conflict between Unites States military forces and American Indians took place not out West, as one might think, but in Minnesota, on the shores of Leech Lake in the summer of 1898.

The Ojibwa are still here and are profiting from legalized gambling on the state's reservations. Starting with small-scale bingo games in the early 1980s, the industry has grown into today's casinos built alongside huge parking lots filled with cars and pickup trucks and charter buses from far and near. Some call these multimillion-dollar casinos "the new buffalo." The casinos bring work to places that have always lacked jobs, but they also bring the temptation of looking for the big rainbow, the winning jackpot. Some reservation members get hooked.

Along with the new buffalo is a resurgence of the Ojibwa's culture. On Memorial Day of 1991 I went to a powwow at the Cass Lake Ojibwa reservation. Indians from Minnesota and other states had campsites nestled beneath pine trees near the dancing grounds. An announcement was made that there would be a special dance in honor of a young Lakota from near the North Dakota border who had been killed in the Gulf War. He had been the first casualty from Minnesota. A young Indian man standing next to me was looking at something in the clear blue sky above us. I followed his eyes and noticed a dark blur of motion that quickly skidded out of sight beyond the timberline.

"That was an eagle—probably him," he said, mentioning the name of the Indian who had been killed a world away from this place in the pines. "He was looking at us."

Weaving my way around campers, tents, and pickup trucks, I walked through the campgrounds at dusk, passing families seated by fires, the licking orange flames just strong enough now to cast shadows. A mother was dressing her small boy on the hood of the family car; a wife adjusted her husband's feathered hair roach. Women in beautifully beaded buckskin dresses with pastel-colored shawls dripping from their shoulders walked together through the trees. Hundreds of metal cones sewn to their dresses made a soft chorus of clattering in passing. From a nearby van where a braided-haired girl examined her face in the rearview mirror came the sound of rap music. From the dancing ground came the sound of drums.

Powwow, Cass Lake

58

Powwow, Cass Lake

Powwow, Cass Lake

Powwow, Cass Lake

Minnesota Historical Society Forest History Center

It was the logging and railroading boom period of the late nineteenth century that truly opened northern Minnesota and eventually led the region to its present economic base of recreation.

I grew up to the sound of waltzes and polkas. My father played accordion—the old button-type—and my mother played piano. They performed—not terribly well—at Scandinavian lodge dances, and I would sometimes go with them to watch the couples swirl and two-step in the close, hot air of the hall. I remember the women in their summer dresses and the men, some of them farmers, with their bronzed faces and flesh-white brows. When the men danced, the backs of their shirts were tight and slick with sweat. They were working-class people, some of them born, like my father, in another country.

My father immigrated to Minnesota from Sweden in 1903 when he was four. His father came looking for cheap land to farm north of the growing cities of Minneapolis and St. Paul. Up in the lake country it was cheapest, but much of that land had already been harvested hard of one crop—trees. Now the trees were gone and northern Minnesota would become, as a University of Minnesota publication of the time predicted, an "agricultural utopia." At least that's how it was supposed to be. It didn't work out that way, and my grandfather was lucky he settled for a quarter section of prairie land north of the Cities but short of what had been the north woods. A lot of men went broke trying to farm up there after the lumber barons had taken their wealth from the forests, leaving a graveyard of stumps behind.

It was the logging and railroading boom period of the late nineteenth century that truly opened northern Minnesota and eventually led the region to its present economic base of recreation. Sixty-eight *billion* board feet of lumber —most of it white pine—was produced in northern Minnesota between 1830 and 1930.

According to Skip Drake, site manager for the Minnesota Historical Society's Forest History Center in Grand Rapids, with its recreated 1900-era logging camp, prior to 1900 you could almost be guaranteed a community of loggers from Maine or Canada working Minnesota's north woods. "English and French were the languages," he told me. "But shortly after the turn of the century you'd find a camp bunkhouse filled with immigrants right off the boat: Germans, Dutch, Polish, Irish, Finns, Norwegians, and Swedes. Some had no idea what they were doing in the woods. It might be their very first job in America."

They logged the north woods only in winter—or, better yet, *despite* the winter, as brutal as Minnesota winters can be—with teams of massive draft horses hauling two-story loads of timber out on sleighs over manmade icy ruts that functioned like railroad tracks to support the runners of the sleighs. Logging season ran from early November to the end of February.

Of all the jobs in a logging camp, perhaps none was more important than that of camp cook, who was usually, but not always, a woman past "marrying age," which meant from about fourteen to the mid-twenties. Assisted by a "cookee," the cook was responsible for feeding close to eighty men three times a day. The morning and evening meals would be served in the cookhouse; lunch would be sent out to the men in the woods. Every morning, seven days a week, the cook would start work two hours before sunrise; quitting time was two hours after sunset. For fifty dollars a month. Cookees got twenty-five, loggers made thirty.

Becky Risse is a thirty-six-year-old housewife from the Grand Rapids area. During the summer she plays the role of logging-camp cook Rebbeca Affield, explaining her job to tourists at the history center. As Miss Rebbeca she wears a pocketed apron over a blouse and full-length skirt. Her hair is in a light brown bun. Wire eyeglasses frame bright eyes on a small oval face that smiles gently as she explains rules of the cookhouse with an authority that suits a woman whose domain is indisputable. Becky does this four days a week for the three-month summer season. The rest of the year she concentrates on the care of her three teenaged children.

Becky tells the tourists that the loggers called pancakes "sweat pads" because they soaked up syrup like the pads on a horse collar soaked up sweat. Biscuits were called "sinkers." Everything was washed down with coffee, or tea, called "swamp water."

"I do all the bakin' and all the bossin'," she tells the group. "I've gotta feed seventy-six men. They're only allowed in here for about fifteen minutes and I don't allow 'em to talk. If they're talkin' they're not eatin'. Sit down, shovel in the food, and out. Kinda like Christmas dinner, don't ya see. Cook all day and then in fifteen minutes they're done and you're left with a pile of dishes."

Loggers ate a lot of beans and potatoes. Becky talks about the lack of fresh foods in the logging camps. "I don't see any fresh meat out here," she says. "Think I see any fresh eggs? Grand Rapids is two days from here. I don't think they'd make it. They'd probably freeze and break."

"Every day I bake twenty-four loaves of bread and thirty pies. Every morning I make five hundred sweat pads. And I make sure there's loggin' berries three times a day. Ya know what those are, don't cha? Prunes. Beans and spuds and loggin' berries. Ya saw the outhouse out there? There might be an inch of ice on that outhouse log in the morning, and you don't want to be spending much time out there reading Sears Robuck catalogues."

Meat in a logging camp meant salt pork, salted beef, and for Christmas dinner, salted turkey. But on Christmas the cook promised every man a pie of his own, from a choice of apple, called "pregnant woman" pie because of the way the dried apples swelled up when soaked in water, or apricot, or lemon, sometimes called "shoe pac" pie because if the filling was over-cooked it would turn to a substance resembling the rubber soles of a woodsman's boots.

Looking through a cookhouse book, I came across the ingredients for a "New England Boiled Dinner." Nothing fancy, it simply calls for sixty pounds of ham, forty pounds of cabbage, forty pounds of potatoes, twenty pounds of beets, and ten pounds each of carrots and turnips.

Becky spent the morning grinding coffee beans, drawing water, greasing pans, and lifting a twenty-pound oven door over and over. Just before I left she drew from her apron a pocket watch, its plainness and simple shape seeming to be a symbol of the period, the place, and a lack of pretension. And yet, according to Miss Rebbeca, perhaps not. "This was not a place where time meant much," she said. "Time was really, 'can see, can't see,' dawn til dusk. People up here might have owned a watch but not be able to tell time. The watch might not have even worked."

On another day as I wandered through the recreated logging camp that represents such a vital piece of northern Minnesota history, I experienced a wistful feeling of times past. In the horse barn where they keep a Percheron draft horse like the ones that hauled fortunes from the forests, a man dressed as a logger sat on a hay bale, strumming a guitar and singing to himself, waiting for tourists. The melody, so soft but clearly recognizable, was like the voice of an old friend to my ears: "Halsa Dem Darhemma—Greet Them at Home," one of the best-loved immigrant songs of Scandinavian Americans, a lilting waltz from my childhood. The horse stood idle, halter tied to a manger, his silky tail fending flies. For a few minutes I stood listening in that barn, seeming empty of anything but the man, the horse, the music, and me. But, in fact, the barn was full of memories, and I was home.

Looking through a recipe book I came across the ingredients for a "New England Boiled Dinner." Nothing fancy, it simply calls for 60 pounds of ham, 40 pounds of cabbage, 40 pounds of potatoes, 20 pounds of beets, and 10 pounds each of carrots and turnips.

Becky Risse, camp cook, Minnesota Historical Society Forest History Center, Grand Rapids

TIME AT THE LAKE

Will Hollnagel and "Doc," Minnesota Historical Society Forest History Center, Grand Rapids

Anthony and Paul
Bunyon, Brainerd

Birch trees and yard deer, Highway 2, Deer River

TIME AT THE LAKE

Resort owner, Ted Leagjeld

It was from some of the clear-cut forest land and some of the early failed farms that the first fishing camps and resorts were established in northern Minnesota. "After they logged off a lot of this country," one man told me, "people said, 'Hey, you can see the lakes now,' and started building cabins along the shore." In the beginning, as someone once said, it was just "bad roads and good people."

Resorts, at least the smaller ones I used to know, were always mom-and-pop businesses. Twenty years ago there were around 2,500 resorts in the state. Today that number has dwindled to about 1,200. "Land has simply become too expensive," Ted Leagjeld said at Driftwood on Upper Whitefish Lake, one of the oldest resorts in the state. "The mom-and-pop resorts with just a few units have become worth much more when sold as individual cabins. The big resorts are getting bigger, and the small ones are disappearing. We're a bit more than twice the size we used to be."

The Leagjelds offer pony rides and an antique fire engine, as well as golf, tennis, and a swimming pool. "People are just looking for relaxation and fun," says Ted. "Right from the beginning we were less fishing and more family-oriented. You can't bring Aunt Bessie up and plant her in a cabin all day." Many other resorts have begun to turn away from a fishing emphasis to activities designed to lure a greater variety of visitors—and for shorter, but more frequent, vacations.

All through the lake country I met people who are trying to make a go of the resort business, a way of life that represents a dream to some but comes with all the demands of reality for those who live it.

Ted Leagjeld, owner, Driftwood Resort, Upper Whitefish Lake

Resort owners, Greg and Shirley Geiger

In their early fifties, Greg and Shirley Geiger have run Trail's End, a nine-cabin resort on Bowstring Lake near Deer River, for about fourteen years. Working out of Minneapolis, Greg had traveled for a major cosmetics company for fifteen years before he and Shirley decided to buy Trail's End, after looking at seventy-five different places over two years. Both of then knew that running a resort was going to be a lot of hard work. But they don't really look at it as a "lifestyle," as one so often hears up here.

"A way of life?" says Shirley. "We don't accept that attitude. We *won't* accept that. From the beginning we both wanted to run this like a business. This is our *job*."

"In some ways," says Greg, "it does become harder each year. State and county regulations become difficult to deal with. We have the same criteria to meet as does a Holiday Inn in the city. And you've got to change and improve or you're not going to stay in the industry. If you don't upgrade continually you aren't going to make it."

The Geigers have raised two sons at Trail's End. The older, a twenty-seven-year-old, now lives in Wisconsin; the younger, fourteen-year-old Michael, helps with the resort during the summer months when school's out.

"We didn't buy this place just to enjoy, but to run as a business," says Shirley. "We have been able to make a very good living, and we have the bonus of being able to live together as a family. We're a very family-oriented couple. This has been perfect."

Greg (far left) and Shirley Geiger, owners, Trail's End Resort, with son, Michael, Bowstring Lake

"Fathers and Kids"
bass tournament,
Leech Lake

Bass tournament, Cedar Lake

"Take a Kid Fishing" day, Lake Bemidji

"Take a Kid Fishing" day, Lake Bemidji

"Take a Kid Fishing" day, Lake Bemidji

Lower Hay Lake

Cop from Chicago

In Nisswa I met Reggie Chisholm, a cop from Chicago. He and his wife, Johnye, a school teacher, come to northern Minnesota each year to fish Lake Hubert, a very good bass lake. He told me about a nice fish his wife caught. "Johnye got this three-pound small mouth and she was gonna release it. I told her, 'No, wait, I'll run in to Wal-Mart and get a camera and a scale.' So we put the bass in the live well, we dock the boat, and I take off for Wal-Mart. Forty-five, fifty minutes later I get back and she says, 'I've changed my mind.' So now I got a fifty-dollar camera, a forty-dollar scale, and it's gonna cost me a hundred and seventy-five to mount that fish."

Checking in a bass at Marv Koep's, Nisswa

Loons

The common loon—a mediocre name indeed for such a marvelous creature—is Minnesota's state bird and can be found on most of the lakes over fifty acres in size. Loons are simply wonderful in the water, and, best of all, they make music. At least it is music to my ears, and to those who are so affected by the haunting repertoire of calls that they move to northern Minnesota to be with them. Perhaps their sounds remind us that this land was once truly wild and untouched by human hands, and they show us that if we are simply quiet and listen, there is still peace to be found in these mirrored waters.

I can't possibly remember when I first heard a loon because I would have been an infant. But I can remember years of hearing them from gently rocking boats with a scrim of early morning fog between me, the rising sun, and the rest of the world, or on a shoreline in the depth of night while northern lights played their magic across the sky and my mind; some way, somehow, I was always hearing those sounds as if for the first time.

The sounds of the loon are impossible to adequately describe; they must be heard. According to novelist and poet Jim Harrison, the call of the loon and the coyote are related, "if only spiritually." For some, however, the sounds of loons might be too intense. My favorite description of a loon call is writer John McPhee's characterization of the tremolo, the loon's all-purpose call, signifying everything from a greeting to worry to alarm. "If he were human," said McPhee, "it would be the laugh of the deeply insane."

Loon on its nest,
Leech Lake

Personal watercraft

Lake pollution comes in many different forms. Personal watercraft (PWC) pound across the lake like aquatic snowmobiles and can be dangerous to operators and boaters alike if not run with caution, and they make a particular kind of noise that is not listened to favorably by many lake lovers. Their protests have resulted in regulations prohibiting PWCs from being operated on a lake between sunset and sunrise. At least that's the law. Enforcing those laws, of course, is another matter in a land of more than ten thousand lakes.

Like the sound of loons, the sound of a PWC is difficult to describe. A loon makes a sound of seclusion, if not, in fact, wilderness, and a PWC seems able to break that seclusion from far, far away. Those old enough to remember might find the sound reminiscent of the old-style dentist's drill, the kind with lots of belts and pulleys, the kind that didn't always have constant power but would surge when the dentist stepped on the foot pedal. Even when he shot a spray of water splashing against the roof of your mouth, you could still feel the heat that came from the drill bit, and as the sound surged, your instinct was to pull your head back, and the muscles in your forearms would tense. The sound of a PWC kind of reminds me of all that. Of course, you have to be middle-aged to remember such a thing, I suppose, and you don't see many middle-aged folks on PWCs.

Sheriff's deputy warning PWC users, Lake Pokegama

Polka festival

In years past you could find a polka band in just about every crossroads tavern in northern Minnesota; today you have to search hard to find any. "It's all rock and roll now," said an accordion player I came across at a polka festival near McGregor, held in a barn converted to a dance hall. The dancers were all middle-aged or older. The men wore polyester pants, and the women swirled around the dance floor in skirts shorter than their ages seemed to call for.

"Some of these old guys are in their eighties, and they don't miss a dance," said a man wiping sweat from his brow and gulping down a beer. "My God," he said, "I can't do it. I smoke, and I'm all done after about a waltz and a half."

A lot of the dancers were members of the Polka Lovers Klub of America (Po. L. K. of A.). Somebody told me that the Minnesota chapter was the "mother club," but other state chapters had dropped out of the organization because of "too much arguing." Just what is happening to this country, I wondered, if there is dissension among the polka lovers?

Ed, the "polka prince," Larson's Barn, McGregor

Resort marriages

People get married at lake resorts; sometimes the couple may even have first met at the resort when they were kids. One young North Dakota farm couple I met at Madsen Grove Resort on Little Floyd Lake, near Detroit Lakes, told me they'd gotten married at the resort, although they hadn't met there. The young groom-to-be had been hoping to marry into the farm family he worked for, but was not an experienced farmer himself. The week he intended to ask the girl's parents' permission for her hand in marriage, he drove the farm pickup truck into the shop wall, drove the tractor through a fence, and rolled over a grain truck with a family relative inside. "I figured if they said no, it was only because they were mad at me," he said. But the parents gave their consent, and after the wedding the bride and groom went water-skiing, he in his tux and she in her bathing suit and bridal garter.

Two girls at a wedding, Rice Lake

Balloon stomp, Kee-Nee-Moo-Sha Resort, Woman Lake

Greased watermelon polo, Kee-Nee-Moo-Sha Resort, Woman Lake

Woman Lake

Kee-Nee-Moo-Sha Resort, Woman Lake

Grand View Resort, Gull Lake

94

Kee-Nee-Moo-Sha Resort, Woman Lake

Dinner time prayer, Madsen Grove Resort, Little Floyd Lake

TIME AT THE LAKE

Madsen Grove Resort, Little Floyd Lake

Cafe scene, Detroit Lakes

Every weekday morning men cluster around tables cluttered with coffee cups at the Main Street restaurant in Detroit Lakes. A lot of them are white-haired, and some wear hearing aids. They slide their cups back and forth between their hands, hunched over at times as if in some kind of local conspiracy. They talk a lot about old times, the sound of old outboard motors, and, quite often, their fathers now long dead. They laugh a lot, reason enough at any stage in life to gather together when you can.

One morning they are talking about a member of the community who has just died after a long illness.

"Well, you know, I went over to the funeral home to see Carl," said a man dressed in blue coveralls. "God, he really looked good."

"Well, hell, he should have," said another in the group. "He just got out of the hospital."

The talk turns to an item in the Minneapolis paper about a purse snatcher who was run over by his victim after she followed him in her car.

"Well," said one of the men, "did you hear about the woman over here who ran over herself?" He waved a big calloused hand toward the street just outside the restaurant window. His friends looked at him kind of blankly, obviously not recollecting this event.

"Oh, yeah," he said, "she and her husband were parked over there and she wanted her husband to go across the street and get something for her but he wouldn't go, so she ran over herself."

"Oh," said one of the men, "yeah?"

"She ran over herself," the first man repeated.

"Yeah?" said another.

"Takes a while to catch on sometimes, don't it."

"Oh . . . yeah."

A waitress, easily young enough to be a granddaughter to anybody in this bunch, came over to clear away a few plates and utensils. "How was everything?" she asked a bald man in a red windbreaker. He didn't respond. Didn't even look at her. She tried again. "Is everything all right this morning?" she said brightly. The man turned his head away from her, turning the other side of his head, the side with the hearing aid even farther away from her inquiring face. "Golly," he said to his friends, propping his elbows up on the table, his arms splayed out into the space made available by the waitress, "you guys always take more room at the table 'cause you eat so much stuff. I don't eat so much stuff. I might though if the waitress would come around more often, and I sure could use some more coffee about now."

Morning of muskie tournament, Walker

100

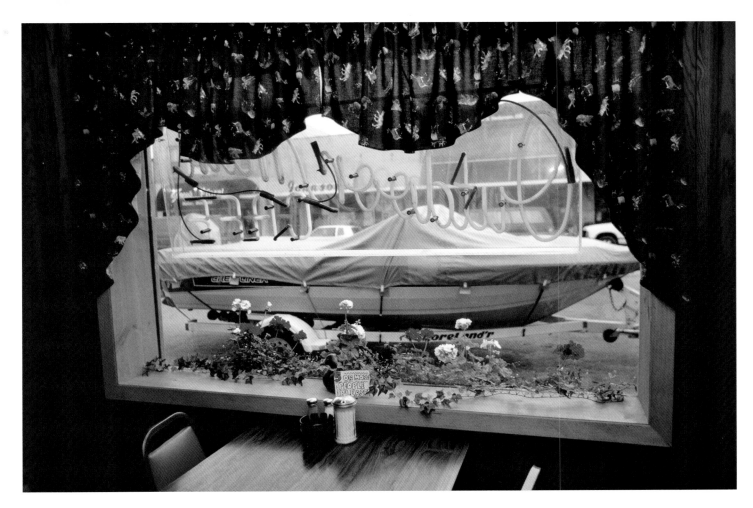

Outdoorsman Cafe, Walker

Severe weather/Al Maas and his sons

Nothing about Minnesota weather is as typical as its ability to change dramatically and fast. Heavy weather can come with tragic surprise. The snows and savage blizzards don't always come in the depths of winter, but sometimes just arrive early, like unexpected guests when your house is not in order, like the blizzard of early November 1940, which killed fifty-nine people, including fourteen duck hunters. Although lake country is not as prone to tornados as are other areas of the state, the thunderstorms that sweep across the lakes in summer sometimes carry tornados in their midst. The tornados buck away from their entourage of black angry clouds to twist down out of the sky like God's original Mixmaster, guaranteed to wreak havoc, but with no promise of exactly where.

I saw some of these storms batter the lake country during a particularly rough two-week period in midsummer, when dark-clouded rumblings had been part of our days and nights, with lightning so bright and intense that it appeared not so much in the distance as in your face.

I watched a storm move across Gull Lake, darkening the water to ink black. Guests at resorts along Highway 371 stood somber-faced outside their cabins, watching the twister touch down in the distance, then rise again to dance across the horizon. The rain came hard, driven by winds of sixty to seventy miles per hour.

The tornado devastated property in the area and caused one death. Trees that had withstood nature's tribulations for generations were, in a moment, uprooted like garden plants.

After the storm I talked to a man who lived along the highway where the tornado had touched down. His yard was a maze of downed trees and splintered lumber. The garage had been sheared off from the house, and the wall where it once joined the house was plastered with uncountable specks of green from blowing leaves and debris. But he really didn't talk much about losing the garage.

"The trees," he said quietly, "God, I had some beautiful trees."

Unexpected winds, perhaps more than anything else, are feared by fishermen, duck hunters, and anyone who knows and uses the large, relatively shallow lakes that can turn from calm to tumultuous far too quickly sometimes for safety, not to mention comfort.

I went muskie fishing with guide Al Maas on Leech Lake one blustery August morning, the kind of day when fishing should be good because a storm front was due. "Their metabolism speeds up with oncoming storms," Al said, "and they just want to feed, feed, feed."

Maas, in his fifties, is a former biology teacher at the Walker high school. He's a solidly built man with a face reddened by the sun and wind, and bearded, of course, as all fishing guides up here seem to be. His sleek fishing boat was powered by a 150-horsepower motor, and we seemed to fly across the lake.

As we fished the almost 113,000-acre lake Al knows so well, he mused about his experiences as a fishing guide over more than thirty summers and the mystique of muskie fishing.

"I once went twenty-eight straight days with twenty-eight muskies," he said. "I feel bad about that now. You know, in the early days we were all so macho about catching fish."

"I took a pig farmer from Iowa out once, trying for muskies. First cast he caught a thirty-five-pounder. He never said a thing, just got kinda white in the face. 'You okay?' I asked. 'Yeah,' he

Unexpected winds, perhaps more than anything else, are feared by fishermen, duck hunters, and anyone who knows and uses the large, relatively shallow lakes that can turn from calm to tumultuous far too quickly.

said, and didn't say another word until we got to the resort, and then he started hollering. We stood on the dock and he collapsed."

"I've had 'em faint, have heart attacks . . . "

We didn't have any luck that day, although we did have a couple of "follows"—muskies that appeared just beneath the surface of the water, following our lures in until just a few feet from the boat, and then were gone like ghosts. Even though we weren't catching fish I could see other boats following ours, knowing that Al Maas was a muskie hunter worth watching.

"Five boats used to be a crowd out here," said Maas. "Now they're everywhere."

Fifteen years ago, Al Maas lost two of his own children to Leech Lake. His only sons, ages nineteen and twenty-one, and a companion, a resort owner, were drowned when their duck hunting boat capsized in a sudden, unexpected early November storm. Their bodies were not recovered until spring.

Al and I drank the last of the coffee from our thermoses. The wind got stronger, the water chopping up and thumping at the boat that somehow felt smaller now, more vulnerable than when we had put in at dawn.

"I've lucked out at times," he said, looking out at the vast sweep of water surrounding us. "I've come off this lake at times when I shouldn't have made it. And I've lost friends who didn't come off lakes when they should have."

"It happened the first week in November," he said. "We still went to the deer stands when the season opened. I didn't hunt. But I do now."

"I decided my lifestyle wasn't going to change. We had the quality years with those boys, I guess. But a doubleheader—you don't antici-pate that. I think about it still."

Tornado, Gull Lake

Muskie fishing

I once met a man in a northern Minnesota bar who insisted there is a definite common denominator to stories about fishing and sex. "They're all based on lies," he said. I believe that rings a bit too cynical and prefer an observation by the writer N. Scott Momaday, who said, "Man tells stories in order to understand his experience, whatever it may be."

Although fishing stories abound in Minnesota, one fish in particular, unlike anything else that swims in the lakes or rivers of the state, seems to bring out a sense of drama and a need for the telling of tales: the muskie.

The warship of freshwater fish, with its scowling face, underslung jaw, and bucket full of needles for a mouth, the muskellunge looks lethal and is, reigning at the very top of its world, king of the food chain, fearing nothing that swims and showing little respect for either humans or their boats. The state record for a muskie is fifty-four pounds. That fish—caught in 1957 in Lake Winnibigoshish—was fifty-six inches long. Just a bit under five feet.

Over the years the insides of muskies have revealed everything from fish half their size, to ducks, to unopened but very shaken up cans of beer. Almost anything in the water is fair game for a muskie.

The muskie is known as "the fish of ten thousand casts," meaning that you don't go out and catch "a mess of muskies," as one might refer to the pursuit of sunfish or crappies. This is a big-game fish. This is a fish that ought to have an exclamation point after its name. The lakes are full of anglers still looking to catch their first one. Or at least their first big one.

On a dry but hot and humid week in July 1955, Leech Lake became legendary in Minnesota fishing history when over a hundred muskies—many of them weighing between twenty-five and fifty pounds—were caught in what became known as "the muskie rampage."

Looking at photographs taken that week of the rampage, one sees twenty-five muskies hanging in a row before a line of proud and smiling men; one sees muskies stacked in a wheelbarrow like cordwood. All those fish were killed. Today many, perhaps the majority, of those fish would be released to thrill the hearts of others another day. Probably no other fish in Minnesota is more dependent on the practice of catch-and-release for its survival. And no other fish seems to stir the emotions of anglers as does the muskie. It turns fishermen into addicts—muskie addicts. Some say there is no cure.

"I've got muskie fever," said Steven Stetz. An eighty-four-year-old businessman from Kansas when I met him in 1991, Stetz and his children had been coming to Birch Villa Resort on Cass Lake since 1949. "You get that damn muskie fever," he said, "and you just don't get over it." I went out on the lake with Stetz and his son to watch them fish for muskies.

"Hit it . . . hit it." they both spoke out to unseen fish, using both arms, casting out huge lures, again and again, casting and retrieving, casting and retrieving. A heron flew low over our boat, its beating wings sounding like broom strokes on a porch floor.

Stetz talked about muskies he'd caught in the past, recalling the one that danced its way to freedom. "That fish came out of the water, sat on its tail and came straight to the boat . . . fifteen, twenty yards, all on its tail, just dancing. It hit the trolling motor and went right by the boat another ten feet or so and the lure pulled out. The lure came out and hit the guide smack in the ass. You've just got to set that hook immediately and don't give 'em an inch of slack or they'll throw the lure."

"And you sure as hell don't want them to dance," added his son.

They had no luck while I was with them, and as we headed back Stetz talked about the old days at the resort, which he said hasn't changed much. "The cabins are mostly the same," he said. "Erosion has taken some of the beach, but you can see that it's still a kid's paradise . . . they can go out a hundred yards in shallow water . . . beautiful sand."

"In the old days there was just a central shower," he recalled. "We used to take 'possible baths.' You know what they are, don't you? You wash down as far as possible and then you wash up as far as possible. And then you take care of the rest whenever possible."

Back at Birch Villa I met other families who had been coming to the place for generations. The beach indeed seemed a child's paradise, large enough for freedom, small enough for intimacy, with borders to explore. On the beach, four or five mothers were gathered, their children scattered out in perpetual motion. The light of dusk was softly generous to the women. In their thirties and forties, they swatted mosquitoes and talked about their children.

The resort has a small store where everyone sits at night to talk, where mothers looking for relief bring their children to pick out treats of pop and ice cream. On the wall opposite the counter is an array of Polaroid snapshots of resort guests and the fish they caught, the weights and dates. Boisterous men with sometimes supportive, sometimes sardonic, wives sat talking about muskies. A calendar and reservation sheet was behind the counter, and one couple from Chicago with thirteen summers at Birch Villa leaned on the counter, checking their reservations for next year. They spent their honeymoon here and long ago outgrew that cabin.

"Those first years," the wife said, "when the kids were small, I hated it with a passion . . . the trip out here . . . for the next ten days I had to sit in a cabin while my husband fished. I don't call this a vacation anymore. It's a pilgrimage. We'll come up here forever."

Muskie fever.

Al Maas and Bill Diedrich, muskie tournament, Leech Lake

TIME AT THE LAKE

Checking in a muskie, Reed's Sporting Goods, Walker

Muskie tournament, Leech Lake

Resort owner, Effie Ritsche

Effie Ritsche was born on the tenth day of the tenth month in the year 1910, and in 1939 she and her husband, Adolph, an electrician, started Madsen Grove Resort on the edge of Little Floyd Lake, a little more than a couple of hundred acres in size. A bit stooped with age, Effie is about four-feet-eleven-inches, white-haired, and very energetic. "I used to be five-two," she says, in a snappy, matter-of-fact voice. "I'm getting closer to the earth all the time. Soon I'll be six feet under."

Effie's father was a violin maker from Norway who immigrated to Wisconsin, hiring on to work in the north woods there before coming to northern Minnesota to start his own sawmill. "At twelve years old I was cooking for twenty sawmill workers," she says. "I baked twenty-seven loaves of bread three times a week. When I was fourteen I walked eighteen miles to town with six quarters in my pocket, looking for a job." She stayed in a hotel that night for a quarter and the next day found a job taking care of two children in a big house in Detroit Lakes. "They put me up in the attic with the mice and rats and paid me three dollars a week. I saved my money and had my tonsils out. It cost me thirty-five dollars. I worked my way through high school. I got interested in flying and used to go out to the airport where they gave rides for a penny a pound. Much later, when I was sixty-five, I started taking flying lessons. I was gonna be the 'flying grandmother,' but it got too expensive."

After high school Effie went on to get a college degree and taught in a one-room country school. She has written and self-published several books about her experiences and also some poetry. She and her husband were partners in a successful electrical appliance business in Detroit Lakes, and in 1939 Effie took money from her share of the company profits to buy some lots along the undeveloped shoreline on nearby Little Floyd Lake. "It was all brush and beer bottles, with just one shack," she says. "I bought the first lot for thirty-five dollars."

Then she bought a few more. "I traded electrical appliances from our business in return for lumber to build the first cottages." Effie says she did all the electrical work and laid all the linoleum floors from "a roll so big it took six men to carry it." She did all the painting and seeded the grass. She hired a couple to run the resort for room and board. On weekends Effie would work at the resort cleaning cottages and clearing brush. Eventually the resort reached its present size of fifteen cottages.

Hard work owning a resort? "Oh, yeah," says Effie. "But there are two places you can get splinters and I'd rather get them in my hand."

Five years ago Effie sold the resort to her daughter and son-in-law, but she continues to work in the resort store, supplying guests with nightcrawlers and leeches and tips on where the best fishing should be. In fifty-six years of resorting Effie has seen a lot. "I've had people from Arkansas ask me what the fish look like, do they have sharp teeth, and are they poisonous?"

She had a car pull in back in the 70s carrying Illinois license plates, and a man emerged with, in Effie's words, "very piercing eyes." In the passenger seat was an attractive young woman. "Just me and my wife," he told Effie, as she showed him a cottage. "The woman had on a wide-brimmed pink hat and she had very long fingernails," Effie recalled. "Why, she looked like something out of *Redbook* magazine, and I thought, what's *she* doing here? I noticed a big piece of canvas covering the back seat area. I asked the man to register and I assumed he did but it turned out later that he hadn't. He came in the store and bought some bread, milk, butter, and Crisco. That night the couple in the next cottage said to me, 'Those new people are kind of strange aren't they? He went out on the lake tonight with a really big gunny sack.' Well, I didn't think much about it but noticed his boat wasn't in when I went down around nine-thirty to check the boats. My daughter figured he was probably visiting relatives or friends across the lake. The next morning he came in alone and paid my husband for the cottage. We saw the car leaving but we didn't see the wide-brimmed pink hat. When we went into the cottage to vacuum and dust we saw all the groceries sitting on the table unused. The bed was untouched. We never knew just what had transpired that night. We think of it as the 'episode of cottage number four.' "

If Effie is to be believed—and I, for one, find no reason not to—she has experienced more than a few dramatic episodes in her life as a young girl, a young woman school teacher, and someone with fifty-six years in the resort business. "I've been struck by lightning twice, walked through rainbows, been chased by a bear, attacked by a starving bobcat, a timber wolf snagged my skirt, and I've kicked porcupines out of the road. I'm a go-go kind of person." She certainly is, and she's more than willing to explain and describe all episodes mentioned, but they tend to be rather long stories. Effie doesn't have many short ones.

Effie Ritsche, former owner, Madsen Grove Resort, Little Floyd Lake

Kee-Nee-Moo-Sha
Resort, Woman Lake

Madsen Grove Resort, Little Floyd Lake

Madsen Grove Resort, Little Floyd Lake

Kee-Nee-Moo-Sha Resort, Woman Lake

119

Lake Itasca

Night before going home, Kee-Nee-Moo-Sha Resort, Woman Lake

Oak Grove, last resort on Gladstone

Down at the dock the boats were snugged up with pieces of cotton rope or clothesline. An anchor, sometimes made of just an old cement-filled paint can, squatted in its place in the bow and the wooden oars lay along the gunnels. After a rain the boat would need bailing with a coffee can.

When we used to drive up to the lake, the roads would turn to gravel as we drew nearer, then to sand as fine as sugar that would embrace the tires of our Chevy, drawing them in until you could almost feel the wheels being swallowed and the road taking control. Almost there, we would say, looking for the small wooden sign nailed to a tree at the end of a tunnel of pines that perfumed the air and led to another week at a cabin on Gladstone. Almost there.

The cabins we stayed in at Gladstone varied over the years, but they were always what is now called rustic. In the early years there wasn't always an indoor toilet or shower. Trips at night out to those facilities were short adventures in the dark, especially during a thunderstorm, when the lightning seemed so much brighter than it was at home. And on clear nights the northern lights would stream up as straight as floodlights at a movie premiere in the city, or undulate in mystical dance across the sky.

Down at the dock the boats were snugged up with pieces of cotton rope or clothesline. An anchor, sometimes made of just an old cement-filled paint can, squatted in its place in the bow, and the wooden oars lay along the gunnels. After a rain the boat would need bailing with a coffee can. A few translucent fish scales and crinkly pieces of dead worms glistened on the seats.

In years when the entire family could be there together we would gather at night to play cards and tell jokes and laugh until tears came. Everyone in the family loved to compete for a chance to talk and be funny except for my father. He had a keen sense of humor; he just didn't use it as much.

Oak Grove, the resort where my family had last gathered together, and the resort I had most wanted to stay at during my summer of 1991, wasn't there anymore, I discovered to my dismay, early in my wanderings that year. I could barely find where it had been.

Gladstone had always been a private lake with no free public access, which helped keep it less busy, more peaceful. This made it, eventually, more desirable. Other resorts on the lake had been sold off slowly over the years for the cabins and the land, leaving only Oak Grove. Now it too was gone.

I went in search of the owners, Jack and Beulah Szabo, to ask them why. When I found them, just up the road from where the resort had stood, they welcomed me as if I were family. "I knew who you were the moment you got out of the car," said Jack. Like a seldom-seen cousin, I remembered him too. Small resorts tend to make you feel like relatives, if only distant ones.

The Szabos are from Illinois and had vacationed in Minnesota for twenty years before buying Oak Grove, a seven-cabin resort huddled in some hardwoods, in 1973.

"The first time we came up to Gladstone," Jack recalled as we sat at their kitchen table, "I took one trip around the lake and caught about every kind of fish you'd want to catch, and I

thought, this is it. We went back to Illinois, sold our home, then came back here and bought the place."

"We had no business at first because the previous owner had been so dirty. We couldn't get the floors clean. We worked our fool heads off."

But they got the place in shape and business started coming, as it often does for mom-and-pop resorts, through word of mouth of their reputation for being good people who ran a clean place. There is an old saying in the lake country that if you like to fish, don't ever own a resort, because you won't have any time to. But Jack, who worked full-time for the post office, always seemed to find time to go out on the lake with his customers.

"You have to have a job when you own a resort," Jack said. "You only have about a ten-week season. I used to come home from work and I had things that had to be done, but I'd end up taking a boatload of people out about six days out of the week."

"My father stayed on shore, frail, his eyesight and energy gone, his days on the lake now over. We crossed the lake and rounded a point that shielded a small bay. The late afternoon sunlight was golden on the water and on our faces."

Beulah was remembering the old days as she poured coffee for us. "We catered mostly to people who fished," she said. "We had one couple that arrived and the woman was wearing white gloves." She laughed. "I knew they wouldn't stay here when she got out of that car wearing white gloves."

Jack talked with the gravelly voice of a cigarette smoker, and every now and then Beulah would poke him to correct his memory. "No, Jack, no, that's not right." I couldn't help thinking that I had not yet had a discussion with a pair of resort owners, man and wife, who agreed on the exact order of events in their years of running the place.

But what had happened to Oak Grove?

"God, Bill," said Jack, "I couldn't afford to build up, I couldn't do anything. I'm fifty-eight. It was gonna cost me twenty-five thousand dollars for a new septic system the DNR said I had to have. My hands were tied. Three years ago I heard the DNR was looking for a public access on the lake. I told them I was thinking about selling. They said, 'You *are?*' And I said, 'You bet.' "

"When we had a chance to sell it to them, we jumped. The DNR tried to sell the cabins but they couldn't, so they just bulldozed 'em down and took her away."

"All the years we had the place I never let the guides come in here, and some people hollered about that, but I didn't want this lake to get hit hard. You know, this used to be one of the top walleye and northern lakes in the state."

"Yes," I said, "I've seen pictures."

"We sure don't miss the work," Jack said, as I was leaving. "Now we've got time to travel and see our grandchildren. But we miss the customers. People make friendships up here that last. They sometimes get old and sick, but they want to come back to the lake one more time."

"Yes," I said. "I know."

Ten years earlier my mother, my sister, my younger brother, and I had gone out on the lake in a boat together. My father stayed on shore, frail, his eyesight and energy gone, his days on the lake now over. We crossed the lake and rounded a point that shielded a small bay. The late afternoon sunlight was golden on the water and on our faces. As my brother tilled the boat in small, slow circles, we scattered the ashes of my older brother in that calm cove where he used to catch sunnies in five feet of water.

After we had said our good-byes, we motored back to my father at Oak Grove and ate our supper at a table beneath the trees that gave the place its name. The folks would return two more years and then they too were gone.

During my summer's travels around the area, my wife, Ani, and our then three-and-a-half-year-old son, Anthony, came out to Minnesota from our home in Virginia. We took Anthony to Lake Gladstone. As he played in the tall grass that had overgrown the banks, I walked over the barren site of Oak Grove. The sun was low and warm. A pontoon boat with a family aboard crept slowly along the opposite shoreline.

The toe of my boot uncovered bits of red siding from the walls of the cabins embedded in the dirt, a few scraps of shingles from the roofs. I saw the tracks of bulldozer treads. The trees were gone. Even the stumps.

"Papi," said Anthony, "what are you doing?"

"Just looking," I said.

Anthony bounded away toward the lake through grass that almost reached his shoulders. He was a deer, he said. I know, I replied, and followed him to the water, thinking about the feel of clamshells and small stones beneath the soles of my feet and the sight of minnows darting off in swift dark fleets before my eyes when I waded in the shallow and seemingly endless water of my childhood.

Anthony reached the lake and knelt there at the edge, dipping his hands, palms down, into the water where they made small ripples on the surface. The sun was down now, salmon-colored clouds hung low against the horizon.

With the persistence of his age he turned to me to ask again, "What are you doing, Papi?"

"Remembering," I said, "just remembering." He didn't ask me what, and I'm not sure I could have told him.

Anthony at site of Oak Grove Resort, Gladstone Lake

Anthony at Gladstone Lake